# The Beach Boat

Story by Dawn McMillan

Illustrations by Liz Alger

Harry and Dad
ran down the beach.

"I'm going for a swim!"
said Harry.

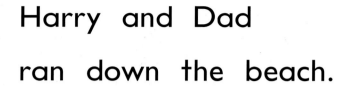

Harry ran into the water.

"Ooh!" he cried.
"The water is **cold**.
It's too cold for a swim."

"We can't go swimming today,"
said Dad.

"Let's make a boat in the sand,"
said Harry.
"Come and help me, Dad."

"Here are the buckets
and spades," said Dad.

"I'm making the inside
of the boat," said Harry.

"And I'm making
the outside," said Dad.
"I will have to get
a lot of sand."

Harry and Dad made a **big** boat.

"This is a very good boat,"
said Harry.
"I'm going to have a ride
in it."

"Come on, Dad," said Harry.
"You can get in the boat, too.
You can sit here."

Dad jumped in,
and sat at the back.

"Dad!" shouted Harry.

"Look out!

Here comes a big wave!

It's coming up to the boat!"

"I'm going to get wet,"
said Dad.

"Look at us!" shouted Harry.
"We are going for a ride
   in the waves!"